CHRISTIANS AT OUR BEST

Christians *at* Our Best

A 6-WEEK GUIDE
TO LIVING IN
THE AGE OF OUTRAGE

ED STETZER
WITH ANDREW MACDONALD

TYNDALE
MOMENTUM®

*The nonfiction imprint of
Tyndale House Publishers, Inc.*

Visit Tyndale online at www.tyndale.com.

Visit Tyndale Momentum online at www.tyndalemomentum.com.

Visit Ed Stetzer's website at edstetzer.com.

TYNDALE, Tyndale Momentum, and Tyndale's quill logo are registered trademarks of Tyndale House Publishers, Inc. The Tyndale Momentum logo is a trademark of Tyndale House Publishers, Inc. Tyndale Momentum is the nonfiction imprint of Tyndale House Publishers, Inc., Carol Stream, Illinois.

Christians at Our Best: A Six-Week Guide to Living in the Age of Outrage

Designed by Mark Anthony Lane II

Published in association with the literary agency of Mark Sweeney and Associates, Naples, FL 34113.

For information about special discounts for bulk purchases, please contact Tyndale House Publishers at csresponse@tyndale.com, or call 1-800-323-9400.

ISBN 978-1-4964-3638-2

Printed in the United States of America

25	24	23	22	21	20	19
7	6	5	4	3	2	1

Contents

Bringing Our Best to a World Engulfed in Outrage

SEVERAL YEARS AGO, Andrew, my coauthor on *Christians at Our Best*, served in a young church that suddenly found itself engulfed in outrage. It had quickly grown from a small church plant meeting in the basement of another church to an established fellowship owning its own property after merging with an older church. As the church continued to grow, the parking lot overflowed each weekend, and many people had to park in the streets of the surrounding neighborhood. To meet the growing need for parking and space, the elders began planning for a building addition.

The first dark clouds warning of an impending storm of outrage were a few handwritten notes local residents left on some members' cars after services. Upset at the vehicles parked outside their houses, the community slowly became more vocal in their anger toward the church. Within a few months, the elders began to hear stories of confrontations between church members and neighbors before and after services.

What had been a minor disagreement erupted into a full-scale war once construction on a building addition was set to begin. On the day the construction equipment was scheduled to arrive so workers could break ground, someone from city hall called to tell the church to halt construction. They had been flooded with calls from the neighbors and were putting a hold on work until they could sort out the problem. Suddenly what had been a small issue affecting a handful of people began to consume every meeting and conversation in the church.

Even more disheartening than the stubborn and mounting hostility from area residents was the reaction of some people in the church. During meetings about the church's future, several people recommended that members respond in kind: to match outrage for outrage. This small but vocal group tried to paint their neighbors as evil—tools Satan was using to stop God's church. Constantly talking about their "rights," they tried to push the church into using every legal and social option to defeat and silence those "opponents of the gospel." As the intensity of the conflict increased, quite a few people simply tried to check out. Their strategy was to ignore the problem, committing to "make do" with their current situation and hoping that the storm would blow over.

Neither attitude proved effective. The conflict dragged on for months as both Christians and non-Christians fed into one another's anger, suspicion, and division. At one point, the level of hostility was so high that an area resident confronted the senior pastor and elders with the threat that the church would expand "over my dead body."

Welcome to the age of outrage.

Perhaps you've had a similar experience within your church or in your local community. Sadly, Andrew's experience is hardly unique. In working to revitalize churches, I frequently sit through meetings in which elders and pastors recount similar stories of outrage. Even in my own writing I am targeted by vitriol and hate for helping Christians make sense of current events. Our world is filled with unprecedented outrage against Christians, by Christians, and most disturbing, by Christians against Christians. In every corner of the Internet, on every cable news program, and even around many family dinner tables, we see people spewing anger and discord. Of course, political and cultural divisions are hardly new. Yet the combination of rapid advances in technology and the shift of Western society into a post-Christian culture seems to have unleashed a wave of outrage.

Certainly problems like terrorism, sex trafficking, abortion, systemic racism, child poverty, political corruption, and opioid addiction rightly capture our attention. Worse yet are those who profess to know Christ but become the center of scandal and controversy, seemingly unaware of how their actions and words are damaging the witness of the church. These issues deserve a measure of outrage, don't they? They certainly deserve our anger.

In moments like these, it is easy to simply join the chorus of angry voices or shrink back into isolation. To become agents of outrage ourselves or to refuse to engage at all.

For many of us, the constant yelling and finger-pointing gets our blood boiling. Without thinking twice, we jump recklessly into the fray, trading shot for shot with others on social media or in the line at Starbucks.

Most of us, however, retreat from the anger around us. We see people torn apart in the news, online, or in real life for having views and beliefs similar to our own, so we shy away. Or we ourselves have been burned by an outraged culture and vow "never again." Not wanting to be branded as intolerant by some or as heretics by others, we choose simply not to engage.

There is a better way. At this critical time, we need to remember Christ's encouragement and exhortation that he has "overcome the world" (John 16:33). No matter how chaotic and angry our culture becomes, God continues to reign through the redemptive work of Christ, and he is establishing his Kingdom. This insight informed the apostle Paul's simple question in Romans 8:31: "If God is for us, who can ever be against us?"

As Christians, we need to consider what it means to be salt and light in our age. Whether we face outrage *toward* Christians, outrage *by* Christians, or simply outrage *at* the outrage, how can we show and share the love of Jesus in a world whose brokenness and pride so often lead to division, self-interest, and offense? This discussion guide is designed to help you answer such questions. I address these themes further in *Christians in the Age of Outrage*. You do not have to read that book to complete this study, but it will give you a firmer grasp of the material covered.

Each of this guide's six sessions is organized around a question related to the way we engage our world with the gospel. The study is designed to move us from the "what" questions of our beliefs and purpose to the "how" questions related to the way we should live out our faith. In other words, we move from questions of understanding to questions of application:

Session 1: *What do we believe?* Understanding how and why we forge our worldviews

Session 2: *What is our purpose?* Embracing our identity as Kingdom ambassadors

Session 3: *How do we see others?* Developing a winsome love for people

Session 4: *How do we respond to wrongs?* Separating righteous anger from worldly outrage

Session 5: *How do we engage the world?* Aligning our online life with gospel mission

Session 6: *How do we engage our community?* Recognizing the power of thinking locally

A brief video introduces each of these sessions. (The videos are available for purchase at https://edstetzer.com/christians-at -our-best.) After watching it, your group will work through three categories of questions designed to help you engage with our culture. First, you will *reflect* on the video and relevant Scripture passages, discussing their meaning as a group. Second, you will *dig deeper* into the theme of the chapter, developing the central idea as you draw upon your own experiences. Third, you will *respond* by examining your own spiritual walk, considering ways to apply that session's teaching to your life and to better *engage* the world with the gospel. (If you are leading a group through this study, I encourage you to turn to the Facilitator's Guide on page 81 for more information and ideas.)

The age of outrage doesn't benefit from either our hostility or our retreat. It needs Christians to be at our best–courageously and thoughtfully bringing the Good News of Jesus Christ into the midst of the brokenness and pain. This can be both difficult and frustrating, yet that is the calling we have been given by God.

As Andrew's church discovered when many of its neighbors opposed the building's expansion, outrage can lead us to lose sight of our gospel mission. Its neighbors were the church's primary mission field, the people they had initially been so passionate about bringing into their community. By casting them as enemies or simply ignoring them, many in the church had forgotten what they once believed to be God's call to *this* community. Thankfully, even in the midst of that storm of outrage, the church leaders endured in faithful ministry. In rejecting the anger and apathy that the expansion provoked, the elders patiently won over members of city hall, several of the neighbors, and even workers on the construction crew who had a front-row seat to the conflict. As a result, the church continued to grow until eventually they bought property on the edge of town, where they minister to a new community today.

In the same way, God has called us to endure in the mission of engaging our world, even when it has given itself over to outrage. It is a high calling that deserves our utmost. No matter how much we may want to, we cannot cede the public square to the voices of outrage. We cannot give up, and we cannot give in.

What Do We Believe?

Understanding How and Why We Forge Our Worldviews

- For a deeper understanding of living with a biblical worldview, read chapter 7 of *Christians in the Age of Outrage.*

- The teaching video for this week's session is available for purchase at https://edstetzer.com/christians-at-our-best.

EVERY CHRISTIAN IS CALLED to live in the tension of being in the world yet not of it (John 17:14-16). We are to resist the temptation to believe and live as those who do not know God while also engaging culture rather than isolating ourselves or retreating from it. We are called to be both set apart (1 Peter 2:9) and lights in the darkness (Matthew 5:13-16). The primary way we live out this calling is by ensuring that our worldview is shaped by the gospel even as we speak into a hostile and selfish world.

In this session, we will examine how our habits, our daily routines, and the voices we allow to influence us shape our worldviews for either godliness or worldliness. These same forces also prepare us to either engage with or succumb to the age of outrage.

RECAP AND RESTATE

Use the space below for notes on the key takeaways from the teaching video.

A worldview is a set of _____ _____

that inform the way we _____ and _____

the world. It is the _____ through which we interpret

_____ _____ and _____.

A worldview can be deformed or worldly if it is influenced by . . .

Four categories of gospel-tempered voices that can shape our thinking according to God's truth are

1. _____

2. _____

3. _____

4. _____

The three "ancient paths" or spiritual disciplines that help forge a gospel worldview are

1. _____

2. _____

3. _____

CONSIDER

What is one practice you have adopted over the past few years that has affected your daily routine or outlook on life?

REFLECT

In his letter to the Romans, Paul encourages believers to present their bodies as living sacrifices to God. One practical way we do this is by ensuring that our worldview, the lens through which we see and interpret the world, is shaped by God rather than the culture around us.

I appeal to you therefore, brothers, by the mercies of God, to present your bodies as a living sacrifice, holy and acceptable to God, which is your spiritual worship. Do not be conformed to this world, but be transformed by the renewal of your mind, that by testing you may discern what is the will of God, what is good and acceptable and perfect.

ROMANS 12:1-2, ESV

1. Paul mentions two qualities of our living sacrifice: "holy and acceptable to God." How can we ensure that our worldview is holy and acceptable?

2. Paul calls this act of living sacrifice our "spiritual worship." In what ways does shaping our worldview constitute worship? How can seeing it as worship motivate us to be obedient and faithful?

3. Why is Paul's contrast between *conformed to* and *transformed by* important in understanding the difference between worldly and gospel-shaped worldviews?

One way we conform to the world rather than being transformed by God's Spirit is by following worldly leaders. Scripture repeatedly warns against emulating leaders who serve some other agenda or purpose than God's Kingdom. These voices hold immense power in influencing our worldview, distracting us from the mission God has given to us. This is one of the major themes of the Old Testament prophets, who rebuked Israel for listening to foolish and worldly leaders:

This is what the LORD of Heaven's Armies says to his people:

> "Do not listen to these prophets when they
>> prophesy to you,
>> filling you with futile hopes.
> They are making up everything they say.
>> They do not speak for the LORD!
> They keep saying to those who despise my word,
>> 'Don't worry! The LORD says you will have peace!'
> And to those who stubbornly follow their own desires,
>> they say, 'No harm will come your way!'
>
> "Have any of these prophets been in the LORD's
>> presence
>> to hear what he is really saying?
>> Has even one of them cared enough to listen?"

JEREMIAH 23:16-18

4. How does this passage define false teaching? What common characteristics are there that can help us spot it today? How does worldly teaching differ from godly teaching? (For further background, see Ezekiel 13:4-7.)

5. How did this false teaching affect Israel's worldview? How did it shape the people's relationship to God?

6. This passage tells us the false teachers *claimed* to speak for God. How can Christians discern whether a leader is honestly speaking for God? What role can family, church, and small groups play in helping believers navigate this challenge?

7. In Luke 6:26, Jesus points back to these Old Testament rebukes to judge the Pharisees: "What sorrow awaits you who are praised by the crowds, for their ancestors also praised false prophets." Why does Jesus focus on the popularity of false teachers? Why are we tempted to listen to popular leaders?

Our habits also influence our thinking and perspective. Where we spend our time and energy will either lead us deeper into a knowledge and love for God or conform our minds and behavior to the culture around us. In the video, I single out Scripture reading, prayer, and fasting as three crucial spiritual disciplines needed to combat the encroaching influence of outrage today. These help Christians ensure that their inputs and outputs are oriented toward God rather than this world, while also reminding us that we truly *need* God's presence and provision. Read through the following verses to discover more about each spiritual discipline. Then answer the two questions that follow:

Scripture: Joshua 1:8; Jeremiah 15:16; Romans 10:17

Prayer: Ephesians 3:14-17; Philippians 4:6-7; 1 John 5:14-15

Fasting: Joel 2:12-14; Matthew 6:16-18

8. What do these passages teach us about the disciplines and how God uses them in our lives?

DIG DEEPER

The apostle Paul exhorts believers "to put off your old self, which belongs to your former manner of life . . . and to be renewed in the spirit of your minds, and to put on the new self" (Ephesians 4:22-24, ESV). In other words, more than simply removing the voices of outrage from our lives, we who are believers need to replace them with leaders who are mature in their faith and devoted to building God's Kingdom. I call these "gospel-tempered" voices, leaders in our lives who have chosen to refine their thinking and behavior by the gospel, just as fire tempers metal. In the video, I suggest that Christians need to find four kinds of leaders to follow: *cultural, pastoral, theological,* and *local.* Such leaders help us understand the world, respond to the challenges of life, deepen our faith, and pursue life-on-life discipleship with others.

1. Who are these gospel-tempered voices in your life? Share examples of the ways God has used these leaders (whether through their writing or speaking, or in real-life interactions) to help shape your worldview.

   a. *Cultural:* How have they challenged you to see and engage the world in ways that are in line with the gospel?

b. *Pastoral:* How have they encouraged you to respond to specific trials and challenges in your spiritual walk?

c. *Theological:* How have they deepened your knowledge of God and his Word?

d. *Local:* How have they walked through seasons of life with you and your family? What lessons have you learned from their discipleship?

2. If listening to false teachers is easy and appealing, how can listening to gospel-tempered voices be difficult? What are some ways we can persist in listening to convicting teaching?

In *Christians in the Age of Outrage*, I explore how our daily habits and routines have been profoundly reshaped by technological advances. Most startling, we often don't notice how much of our lives we give to these new habits.

The entertainment industry is always studying ways to
hold our attention for the longest stretch of time. Whether
companies are trying to entice us to go from one show
to the next, one article to the next, or one blog post to the
next, they will not let our attention go without a fight.
The root of the issue is this: *They are fighting for our
discipleship, for our love. . . .*

In a new reality where there is more content than we
can possibly consume, we need to develop the necessary
discipline to recognize the danger in drinking from a
bottomless mug. There is *always* another podcast, *always*
another Instagram post, *always* another television series.

Pages 142–143

In his well-known 1978 book, *Celebration of Discipline*,
Richard Foster noted, "Superficiality is the curse of our age. The
doctrine of instant satisfaction is a primary spiritual problem."[1]
If anything, the "doctrine of instant satisfaction" has become
more of an idol than it was when Foster penned those words.
Christians need to consider how our media habits are discipling
us and shaping our thinking and engagement with the world in
ways we may not even notice.

3. Why is it important to think critically about our habits? How
   can being ambivalent or uncritical hurt our worldview in the
   long run?

4. What does it mean that everyone is "fighting for our discipleship, for our love"? How can we form habits and behaviors that protect us from adopting unhealthy thoughts and actions?

5. What are some ways that Christians can use technology and media (shows, podcasts, social media) to help shape a gospel worldview? What practices and resources do you use that contribute to this worldview?

RESPOND AND ENGAGE

One of the most frustrating realities of ministry is how Christians treat spiritual disciplines. When pastors talk about the value of prayer, Bible study, and fasting, the majority of believers agree. Yet when we look at how frequently these are practiced by people *within the church*, we see that only a fraction of believers engage in them. A recent study found that just 45 percent of people who attend church regularly read the Bible more than once a week. More than 40 percent of church attenders read their Bibles occasionally, about once or twice a month. Almost one in five church-goers say they *never* read the Bible, which is about the same number as those who read it every day.[2]

In other words, even though many Christians acknowledge that spiritual disciplines are essential to their spiritual walk, they don't practice them.

Like the person who wants muscles without working out, we want the fruit of spiritual maturity without the discipline of submitting our thinking and habits to the gospel. But the truth is, if we want a worldview shaped by the gospel, we must incorporate spiritual disciplines into our lives.

1. Why do you think Christians acknowledge the importance of spiritual disciplines but struggle to practice them? What major obstacles have prevented you from practicing one or more of these disciplines?

2. Reflect on a time when you were able to incorporate a spiritual discipline into your life. How did it affect your spiritual walk? How did that difference shape how you saw and engaged the world?

3. Take a moment to think through the habits, disciplines, and influences in your life right now. Then answer the questions below.

   a. What worldly or unthinking habits have you developed? What spiritual disciplines have you developed? How do you think these have shaped or continue to shape your worldview?

   b. Who are some of the *voices of outrage* that you've followed? How have the gospel-tempered voices you identified on pages 7–8 helped counteract these voices of outrage?

PRAYER PROMPT

Before ending, spend time praying about your worldview as well as the habits and influences that have shaped the way you see and engage the world. Ask God to bring conviction about areas that need to change and for his Spirit to bless your efforts to incorporate new spiritual disciplines and gospel-tempered voices into your life.

What Is Our Purpose?

Embracing Our Identity as Kingdom Ambassadors

- For a deeper understanding of what it means to be Kingdom ambassadors, read chapter 8 of *Christians in the Age of Outrage.*

- The teaching video for this week's session is available for purchase at https://edstetzer.com/christians-at-our-best.

SCRIPTURE GIVES CHRISTIANS an evocative and compelling call to become ambassadors for Christ. Forgiven from sin and reconciled to the Father through Christ, we are not to isolate ourselves but rather to bring the gospel–the Good News–to the world. While our nation's ambassadors have many responsibilities, Kingdom ambassadors have three primary functions.

In this session, we are going to look at how we can live out this threefold calling as Kingdom ambassadors in the age of outrage. It takes courage to step out in obedience and fulfill our mission, but "God will make this happen, for he who calls you is faithful" (1 Thessalonians 5:24).

RECAP AND RESTATE

Use the space below for notes on the key takeaways from the teaching video.

First, ambassadors are *sent by a king.* This means . . .

Second, ambassadors are *sent with a message.* This means . . .

The four components of our message are:

1. A _____ and _____ exist

    between _____ and _____.

2. _____ is the _____ of

    _____.

3. The _____ of _____ _____

   is the sole _____ to this hostility and

   division.

4. Our _____ sets us on _____

   as active _____ in the _____

   of others and of all things.

Third, ambassadors are *sent to a foreign land.* This means . . .

The three primary cultural crises affecting the people we are
to reach are:

The crisis of _____

The crisis of _____

The crisis of _____

CONSIDER

Describe a time when you felt like your Christian faith made you
a foreigner in a strange land. How did you respond?

REFLECT

Read the following passage and reflect on how Scripture speaks about our calling as ambassadors of Christ.

> All of this is a gift from God, who brought us back to himself through Christ. And God has given us this task of reconciling people to him. For God was in Christ, reconciling the world to himself, no longer counting people's sins against them. And he gave us this wonderful message of reconciliation. So we are Christ's ambassadors; God is making his appeal through us. We speak for Christ when we plead, "Come back to God!"
> *2 CORINTHIANS 5:18-20*

1. What are some ways in which God makes "his appeal through us"?

2. Describe a time when you shared God's message of reconciliation in Jesus with someone. What were some helpful Bible verses you used to talk about God's offer of forgiveness and salvation?

Let's take a closer look at the three main points as they relate to living as God's ambassadors.

We are sent by a King

A major theme throughout Scripture is that God is our King. In the Old Testament, God is identified as the true ruler of all creation and the one who reigns from heaven. This same language is used in relation to Jesus in the New Testament. Recognizing God as our sending King is crucial to persevering as Kingdom ambassadors in the midst of a culture of outrage. Isaiah 6:1-3, Isaiah 44:6-8, and John 18:36-37 talk about God as our King. After reading these passages, answer the questions below:

3. What attributes or qualities does Scripture ascribe to God in light of his kingship?

4. How do these passages portray our relationship to God as King?

5. How does God's identity as King affect our relationships with other believers and the way we live on mission?

We are sent with a message

One of the central ideas of being an ambassador is that it's not about us. We have a King, a message, and a people to reach. When we focus on our personal mission, message, and needs, we can lose sight of this role as ambassadors and damage our witness. We can begin to preach about ourselves (our political, economic, or cultural perspective) rather than the gospel of Jesus.

Paul summarizes this truth in 2 Corinthians 4:5-6:

We don't go around preaching about ourselves. We preach that Jesus Christ is Lord, and we ourselves are your servants for Jesus' sake. For God, who said, "Let there be light in the darkness," has made this light shine in our hearts so we could know the glory of God that is seen in the face of Jesus Christ.

6. What are some ways that this world confuses our message? How can we begin to confuse *our* message with the gospel?

7. In mentioning that God has shined his light in our hearts, Paul is reminding the Corinthians of their own reconciliation to God. How does your personal experience of forgiveness and salvation shape your witness?

We are sent to people in a foreign land

The final part of being Kingdom ambassadors is to understand those to *whom* we are to deliver God's message of reconciliation. Charles Spurgeon said that Christians who do not engage the world with the gospel are like those who cling to the treasure, ignoring the needs of others: "The world is starving, and they hoard the bread of life."[3] God calls us to go out into the world, engaging people where they are with the gospel.

8. Read 1 Corinthians 9:19-23. What does the passage teach us about seeing and engaging unbelievers (even those who may see themselves as our cultural enemies)?

DIG DEEPER

In *Christians in the Age of Outrage*, I argue that understanding our calling as ambassadors is crucial to engaging the world:

Ambassadors were more than just messengers or heralds. They were representatives with a mission, endowed with the responsibility to engage a different government or culture on behalf of their sovereign. This means they didn't stay home. To accomplish their king's task, they left and lived in foreign countries—studying the culture, learning the language, eating the food, and seeking to build bridges to communicate their king's message with clarity and zeal. . . .

Similarly, Christians study the culture while seeking to understand how the mechanisms of the foreign land are opposed to the Kingdom of Jesus. While doing this, we are given a heart of compassion by God's Spirit for a people who are also far away from home and living unreconciled to him. This is what motivates us to work for the good of others in both spiritual and practical ways.

Pages 170–171

1. As a student of culture, list some idols you've noticed that this world values that are opposed to the Kingdom of Jesus.

2. What are some idols that can be tempting to Christians or the church? When we give in to them, how is our witness affected?

At the root of our age of outrage are three crises affecting many people: lost identity, misplaced purpose, and chronic loneliness.

3. Read through the following verses and consider what Christianity offers to those suffering in each of these areas.

   Lost Identity: John 1:12; Jeremiah 1:5; Galatians 3:27-28

   Misplaced Purpose: Matthew 6:31-33; Philippians 3:7-14; Colossians 3:1-3

   Chronic Loneliness: 1 Corinthians 12:19-27; Psalm 68:4-6; 2 Timothy 4:16-18

Throughout Scripture Christians are identified as being not of the world (John 17:16). This can lead some Christians to assume that unbelievers are our enemies or that we should retreat from the world. That was never Jesus' message. Read Matthew 5:13-16 to discover how he says we should engage with the world.

4. What images does Jesus use to describe Christians as different from the world? How can these images help us understand our mission and witness in the world?

5. How should our righteousness and good works relate to our witness? How can we keep them from devolving into works-based religion?

RESPOND AND ENGAGE

Being effective Kingdom ambassadors requires that we have a heart for the people around us. We see this most powerfully in the example of Jesus in Matthew 9:35-38.

> Jesus traveled through all the towns and villages of that area, teaching in the synagogues and announcing the Good News about the Kingdom. And he healed every kind of disease and illness. When he saw the crowds, he had compassion on them because they were confused and helpless, like sheep without a shepherd. He said to his disciples, "The harvest is great, but the workers are few. So pray to the Lord who is in charge of the harvest; ask him to send more workers into his fields."

Just as a parent with a sick child feels a deep burden to ease their suffering, Jesus' compassion for the lost is described as a gut-wrenching emotion. He sees their *need* and out of love for them wants to relieve it. Christ's love for the people translated into a deep compassion and therefore an engagement that sought to heal their pain, fix their brokenness, and redeem their hearts by reconciling them to the Father.

1. What was Jesus doing that attracted the crowds to him? What does this tell us about our job as ambassadors who have been entrusted with Jesus' ministry of reconciliation?

2. How does compassion for the world's "lostness" help us engage the people in our community and neighborhoods?

3. Jesus urges his disciples to begin with prayer as they consider the lost people around them. How can prayer help us to be better Kingdom ambassadors?

In *Christians in the Age of Outrage*, I suggest that two important ways we can measure whether we have a heart of compassion for people are to consider how often we pray for the lost and how often we share the gospel with them. I point to one study in which Christians were asked a simple question: "In the past six months, how many times have you personally shared with someone how to become a Christian?"

The most common answer was zero, with 61 percent confessing they had not told anyone how to become a Christian in the previous six months.[4] When the question was adjusted to focus solely on times when Christians invited unchurched people to church rather than personally witnessing to them, the numbers weren't much better (48 percent had invited zero people in the past six months).[5]

Page 188

In a different study, this time on prayer, Americans were asked how often they prayed and for what. One of the more disappointing results of the study is that the number of those who say they've prayed to win the lottery (21 percent) is higher than of those who say they typically pray for those of other or no faiths.[6] I'm pretty sure the Lord would be better honored by us praying to win the lost rather than to win the lottery.

4. Ask yourself the same questions:

    a. In the past six months, how many times have you personally shared with someone how to become a Christian?

    b. In the past six months, how many times have you prayed for someone of another faith or no faith to become a Christian?

5. What are some of the obstacles that might prevent you from sharing your faith? From consistently and specifically praying for the lost?

6. As a group, develop next steps to engaging as Kingdom ambassadors in these practical ways:

   a. Share the name of one person you can pray for consistently over the next week to come to faith in Jesus.

   b. Consider any practical needs this person might have. Suggest one or two ways that you can connect with this person over the next month to offer practical help or to begin sharing your faith.

   c. Discuss ways you as a group can encourage and support one another to live out your mission this week.

PRAYER PROMPT

Before ending, spend time praying about your role as Kingdom ambassadors. Ask God for the compassion to see the lostness of this world and for clarity in your calling to share Jesus' message of reconciliation.

How Do We See Others?

Developing a Winsome Love for People

- For a deeper understanding of the winsomeness of Christian love, read chapter 9 of *Christians in the Age of Outrage.*

- The teaching video for this week's session is available for purchase at https://edstetzer.com/christians-at-our-best.

LOVE IS AT THE CENTER of the Christian faith. Jesus summarized the entire Law and the Prophets as God calling us to love: first to love him with our whole being and second to love others as ourselves (Matthew 22:34-40). This love flows from the recognition that God first loved us: He paid the penalty for our sin and redeemed us by his grace. Yet Christians can often be perceived as deeply *unloving*. Instead of standing out in a world increasingly devoted to outrage, many Christians embrace the language of division that defines our culture.

In this session, we'll consider why Christian love that is empathetic and humble and sees God's image in others draws people to him. We'll also consider how outrage gets in the way of expressing that grace to the lost people around us. Though we cannot compromise in our rebuke of sin, we need to understand how profound winsome Christian love is to a broken world.

RECAP AND RESTATE

Use the space below for notes on the key takeaways from the teaching video.

Love that is *empathetic* is . . .

The major obstacle to empathetic love is

Love that is *humble* is . . .

The major obstacle to humble love is

Love that *values others as image bearers* is . . .

The major obstacle to image-bearing love is

CONSIDER

Describe the Christian (family member, pastor, friend, other) in your life who is the most loving. How does this person show love? How does it shape or change others' perception of him or her?

REFLECT

Even people who have never set foot in a church or cracked the cover of a Bible are familiar with the words of 1 Corinthians 13. It seems so many weddings have three elements: bad bridesmaid dresses, dancing to the YMCA song, and a reading on love out of 1 Corinthians 13. That last connection is so widespread that preachers hesitate to speak on this Scripture because it is so closely associated with the romantic love of newlyweds. But take a step back and read the passage again, keeping in mind that Paul is not primarily talking about romantic love but Christian love more broadly.

If I could speak all the languages of earth and of angels, but didn't love others, I would only be a noisy gong or a clanging cymbal. If I had the gift of prophecy, and if I understood all of God's secret plans and possessed all knowledge, and if I had such faith that I could move mountains, but didn't love others, I would be nothing. If I gave everything I have to the poor and even sacrificed my body, I could boast about it; but if I didn't love others, I would have gained nothing.

Love is patient and kind. Love is not jealous or boastful or proud or rude. It does not demand its own way. It is not irritable, and it keeps no record of being wronged. It does not rejoice about injustice but rejoices whenever the truth wins out. Love never gives up, never loses faith, is always hopeful, and endures through every circumstance.

1 CORINTHIANS 13:1-7

1. How does this passage define the love that is supposed to describe Christians? What should be evident in our love? What obstacles or temptations distract us from being loving?

2. Why does Paul say that without love "I would be nothing"? Why does the absence of love destroy our spiritual walk?

3. What qualities of love in the passage do you struggle with most when relating to others? Why have these proven so difficult?

In this session's *Christians at Our Best* video, I argue that one of the most practical ways that our love can demonstrate humility is through the twin virtues of service and forbearance. For Christians, service means putting others' needs before our own. It means sacrificing our time, energy, and resources to give of ourselves in recognition that everything we have has been given to us by God.

Forbearance is a rarer word, but the idea fills the pages of Scripture as Christians are called to bear with others through difficult circumstances, even when we feel wronged or disrespected. To forbear is to adopt a posture of persistent forgiveness, extending grace to others just as God has given grace to us.

Pride wants to destroy both service and forbearance, tempting us to put ourselves first and to jump ship as soon as things become hard or uncomfortable. Read through the following verses, reflecting on how Christians can live out a humble love toward each other and non-Christians.

Humility through service: Galatians 5:13-14; 1 Samuel 12:24; 1 Peter 4:10; 1 Thessalonians 5:14-15

Humility through forbearance: Colossians 3:13; Ephesians 4:2; Romans 3:22-25; 15:1; Philippians 4:5

4. In light of these passages, how can we reveal the winsomeness of Christian love through humble service? Through forbearing with others?

5. Why does pride make service and/or forbearance difficult? Conversely, how does the gospel help break down this barrier?

6. Reflect on times when you served someone or endured with someone in love. What did you do, and how did it open doors to share your faith?

DIG DEEPER

In *Christians in the Age of Outrage*, I outline how disgust destroys engagement and distorts our view of our sin: "Disgust halts any and all engagement. Like a bad odor or a revolting sight, disgust stops us in our tracks and prevents us from getting any closer to someone" (page 203).

Disgust also distorts our view of our own sin. When we feel disgust toward other people, we reveal our attitude toward their sin and brokenness: We think we are worthy and good while they are unworthy and bad. Such an attitude ultimately shipwrecks our mission to the world.

In the video I argue that this attitude invalidates our claims to love. It transforms what should be a gospel-centered love for sinners as potential vessels of God's mercy into a conditional love predicated upon our cultural and political fears. We stand at the edge of our mission field, focused on those to whom Jesus sent us, but telling them to clean themselves up before we can come any closer. This is not Christian love, and as such it is neither winsome nor effective.

1. Reflect on a time when you encountered something disgusting, like a bad odor. How did you respond? How does disgust toward non-Christians (or other Christians) reflect a deformed view of others and ourselves?

2. How does empathetic love toward the lost counteract disgust at sin? How can remembering our own lostness before Christ help shape the way we engage and love non-Christians?

3. Reflect on a community or people to whom you struggle to show empathy. How can disgust seep into your way of seeing them? How well have you engaged and witnessed to this group in light of your struggle?

Genesis begins with the record of God's most important creative act: the making of humanity. After forming and breathing life into Adam, God declared that he had created humanity *in his own image* (Genesis 1:26-27; 5:1-2). When God confirmed his covenant with Noah in Genesis 9, he prohibited murder because it defaced the image of God in man. The biblical truth that God created man in his image is central to the Christian faith. Theologian Christopher Wright describes it this way: "When we look at any other person, we do not see the label . . . but the image of God. We see someone created by God, addressed by God, accountable to God, loved by God, valued and evaluated by God."[7] For this reason, Christians are called to and have a long history of fighting for the dignity and value of every human life regardless of race, age, gender, or nationality.

4. What does it mean that we are made in the image of God? What does this say about our value to God?

5. In what ways should the fact that all people are "created in the image of God" change the way we see others? What does it mean for how we engage those we disagree with? What does it mean for how we engage those who dislike or even hate us?

6. How is image-bearing love superior to the kinds of love this world has to offer? In what ways can loving others as reflections of their Creator meet the craving this world has to be loved and to love? How does seeing others in this light help our witness?

In Mark 10, Jesus encounters a rich young man who wants to know what he must do to inherit eternal life. The man had lived out the Old Testament commandments but still sought out Jesus because he wanted to be sure he wasn't missing something. Mark records Jesus' response:

> Looking at the man, Jesus felt genuine love for him.
> "There is still one thing you haven't done," he told him.
> "Go and sell all your possessions and give the money
> to the poor, and you will have treasure in heaven. Then
> come, follow me."
> **MARK 10:21**

As Jesus demonstrates, winsome love does not mean Christians should not speak hard truths. It was *because* Jesus genuinely loved the young man that he called him to follow him with his whole heart. While love means that we reject self-righteousness and disgust, it does not mean Christians endorse sin.

7. Later in Mark 10, Jesus notes that his teaching for the young man was hard to hear. How can Christians speak hard truths yet still be loving? How can we both call sinners to repentance and have a winsome love like that of Jesus?

8. In the end, the young man didn't follow Jesus *because his teaching was hard.* Describe a time when you were rejected because you advocated a hard teaching, even though you were loving. What was your response?

RESPOND AND ENGAGE

In Scripture, we find Jesus consistently holding in tension a rebuke to sin and a deep and abiding love for the broken and lost. People in every age, country, and culture have found his approach winsome. Read through the following passages, considering how Jesus models love. Then consider how you can live out these qualities of winsome love practically.

Empathy

Hebrews 4:14-16 reminds us that Jesus is not a distant or abstract God who does not understand our trials and struggles. Some translations of Hebrews use the term *sympathize* (ESV) or *empathize* (NIV) to teach us that Christ entered fully into the human suffering that we experience ourselves.

Jesus' example of entering into our world and empathizing with our suffering sets the tone for how we should understand the lostness and brokenness of this world.

1. Why is the fact that Jesus empathizes with our sufferings and trials important? What would be different if he could not empathize with us?

2. Why are people more inclined to draw near to those who can empathize with them? How can you draw upon your own experience and testimony to engage specific people in your community? How does your story of God's redemption demonstrate empathy with where they are now?

Humility

John 13:1-17 tells the story of Jesus washing the disciples' feet. In a stunning reversal of custom, Jesus did what the servant was supposed to do by washing his disciples' feet. Our world so values status and power that serving others in humility seems foreign, if not wrong, to some people. Yet this is what was so winsome about Jesus' love: flipping the world's logic on its head by revealing the value of people over status.

Jesus then asked his disciples to imitate him. Our faith calls us to follow Jesus in being people of the towel rather than people of the pitchfork. People of the pitchfork are fueled by *their* needs and are quick to anger. People of the towel follow Jesus' model: enduring in loving, humble ministry without exception or expectation.

3. In your own words, how would you describe the difference between "people of the towel" and "people of the pitchfork"?

4. Jesus ended the story by calling the disciples to follow his model, promising that God would bless them if they served others in humble love. How have you experienced God's blessing when you were humbly serving others?

5. What are some ways you can live out this humble love by serving others as Jesus did? What specific needs can you meet through your time or other resources?

Image Bearing

In Luke 19:1-10, Jesus models a compelling vision of image-bearing love as he engages Zacchaeus, a chief tax collector. In the story, Zacchaeus is so despised by his community that he is forced to climb a tree to see Jesus. Instead of rejecting the tax collector, Jesus looks past this worldly identity with all its baggage to see the image of God. Where others recoil, Jesus engages, and in so doing radically transforms Zacchaeus.

In a world that constantly bombards us with accusations of our failures, our lack of worth, and our disqualification for its love, God's image-bearing love endures because it is *who we are.* Christ saw Zacchaeus as a reflection of his own glory, buried under the brokenness of sin.

6. How does Jesus demonstrate image-bearing love to Zacchaeus? How can this be compelling in our world today?

7. Reflect on a time when you were shown love in a situation where you felt rejected or when you showed love to someone others had rejected. How did this make you feel? How did this bring about a change of perspective for you or the other person?

8. How can waiting for someone to earn your love become a
   hindrance to your witness? How have you struggled with
   trying to make others earn your love rather than loving
   them as an act of worship to God?

PRAYER PROMPT

*Before ending, spend time praying about how well you love those
around you, both believers and non-Christians. Ask that God would
give you a greater empathy for others, opportunities to grow in
service and forbearance, and the ability to value others as people
made in the image of God.*

How Do We Respond to Wrongs?

Separating Righteous Anger from Worldly Outrage

- For a deeper understanding of how to distinguish outrage from righteous anger, read chapter 4 of *Christians in the Age of Outrage.*

- The teaching video for this week's session is available for purchase at https://edstetzer.com/christians-at-our-best.

IN THIS WORLD, there is no shortage of sin that should incite Christians to anger. However, having looked at the importance of love in engaging a hostile world, we need to recognize that anger can be either an effective tool in building God's Kingdom or a destructive fire that divides and destroys our communities.

In this session, we are going to consider what it means for Christians to be angry at sin and evil. More important, we'll see how to ensure this anger reflects God's holiness and justice rather than the outrage of this world. Such obedience will take humility and self-control, because even anger must be brought into the service of Jesus Christ and his Kingdom.

RECAP AND RESTATE

Use the space below for notes on the key takeaways from the teaching video.

To be a missionary *to* outrage rather than a missionary *of* outrage means . . .

The three defining characteristics of *righteous anger* are:

1. Anger that _____ _____ _____
   things that anger _____.
2. Anger that _____ the way that _____ is
   angry.
3. Anger that _____ to God's _____
   as the _____ _____ .

In contrast to righteous anger, what are the six characteristics of outrage?

1. _____

2. _____

3. _____

4. _____

5. _____

6. _____

CONSIDER

Describe a time when you felt really angry in a righteous way. How was that different from feeling outrage? How was the outcome similar or different?

REFLECT

In the video, I list three defining characteristics of righteous anger that line up with how Scripture speaks of God's anger, wrath, and holiness. Read through the following verses and questions, considering how Scripture presents God's anger and what this means for how we should or should not be angry today.

Characteristic #1: Righteous anger is directed toward things that anger God

> Jesus went into the synagogue again and noticed a man with a deformed hand. Since it was the Sabbath, Jesus' enemies watched him closely. If he healed the man's hand, they planned to accuse him of working on the Sabbath.

Jesus said to the man with the deformed hand, "Come and stand in front of everyone." Then he turned to his critics and asked, "Does the law permit good deeds on the Sabbath, or is it a day for doing evil? Is this a day to save life or to destroy it?" But they wouldn't answer him.

He looked around at them angrily and was deeply saddened by their hard hearts. Then he said to the man, "Hold out your hand." So the man held out his hand, and it was restored! At once the Pharisees went away and met with the supporters of Herod to plot how to kill Jesus.

MARK 3:1-6

1. In this passage, why does Jesus get angry? What was it about his critics that caused him to look "around at them angrily"?

2. Jesus coupled his anger with healing and restoration. How does this inform why and how Jesus was angry? What does this say about the reasons and ways we may be angry today?

3. The passage ends with the Pharisees plotting to kill Jesus. In what ways does righteous anger require courage?

Characteristic #2: Righteous anger mirrors the way God is angry

> The LORD descended in the cloud and stood with him
> there, and proclaimed the name of the LORD. The LORD
> passed before him and proclaimed, "The LORD, the
> LORD, a God merciful and gracious, slow to anger, and
> abounding in steadfast love and faithfulness, keeping
> steadfast love for thousands, forgiving iniquity and
> transgression and sin, but who will by no means clear
> the guilty, visiting the iniquity of the fathers on the
> children and the children's children, to the third and
> the fourth generation."
> *EXODUS 34:5-7, ESV*

4. In this important Old Testament text, what words does God
   use to reveal himself to his people?

5. What is the relationship between God's steadfast love and his
   righteous anger and judgment? What does that tell us about
   our own anger toward others?

6. How does steadfast love help righteous anger be more effective
   than outrage?

Characteristic #3: Righteous anger submits to God as the ultimate judge

For we know the one who said,

> "I will take revenge.
>> I will pay them back."

He also said,

> "The LORD will judge his own people."

It is a terrible thing to fall into the hands of the living God.

Think back on those early days when you first learned about Christ. Remember how you remained faithful even though it meant terrible suffering. Sometimes you were exposed to public ridicule and were beaten, and sometimes you helped others who were suffering the same things. You suffered along with those who were thrown into jail, and when all you owned was taken from you, you accepted it with joy. You knew there were better things waiting for you that will last forever.

HEBREWS 10:30-34

7. How does God's role as ultimate judge inform righteous anger?

8. These verses call us to endure suffering and oppression. How do suffering and endurance change our view of righteous anger?

9. Describe a time when you struggled to let God be the ultimate judge. Why was waiting in faith so hard? What did you learn about God's role as judge in and through the situation?

DIG DEEPER

As we can see, righteous anger is a high calling. Scripture constantly warns us against anger because of its potential to cause lasting damage to ourselves and those around us.

> Put on your new nature, created to be like God—truly righteous and holy.
>
> So stop telling lies. Let us tell our neighbors the truth, for we are all parts of the same body. And "don't sin by letting anger control you." Don't let the sun go down while you are still angry, for anger gives a foothold to the devil. . . .
>
> Get rid of all bitterness, rage, anger, harsh words, and slander, as well as all types of evil behavior. Instead, be kind to each other, tenderhearted, forgiving one another, just as God through Christ has forgiven you.
>
> *EPHESIANS 4:24-27, 31-32*

1. Why does Paul put anger in the list of sins? How is this kind of anger different from righteous anger? Why is it so important to resolve such anger quickly (before the sun goes down)?

2. Take time to think through anger in your own life. What are some ways that you let anger control you? When you let human anger get hold of you, what other sins listed in verse 31 do you struggle with?

3. Paul encourages believers to pursue kindness, tenderheartedness, and forgiveness as a remedy to human anger. How can these virtues help make sure we do not sin in anger? How does God's forgiveness through Christ fit in?

Too often we believe the lie that our anger is righteous, that it is okay to scream and yell because *we are right.* The truth, however, is that most of the time our anger is our sinfulness getting the better of us. In the video, I mention six defining characteristics of outrage. This is "human anger," focusing on our own wants and needs rather than allowing our response to flow from God's righteousness.

4. What do the six characteristics of outrage tell us about the resulting behavior or attitude? How does this run contrary to the righteousness of God?

5. Which of these characteristics tend to show up when you get angry? How has this hurt your relationships with others? With God?

6. Read the accompanying Bible verse for each characteristic below. How can Scripture offer us a better way than outrage?

Disproportionate: Micah 6:8

Selfish: Ephesians 4:2

Divisive: Romans 12:16

Visceral: Colossians 3:13-14

Domineering: Luke 6:31

Dishonest: Ephesians 4:25

RESPOND AND ENGAGE

Christians who stay on the sidelines or aren't willing to speak truth to power lead others to see Jesus and his Kingdom as uncaring toward their brokenness and pain. Apathy at injustice and sin can be equally damaging to our witness as unbridled rage at every perceived slight. In *Christians in the Age of Outrage*, I offer three practical steps for aligning our anger with gospel mission (pages 85–86, summarized here).

- **Be quick to listen and slow to anger.** Proverbs tells us, "People with understanding control their anger; a hot temper shows great foolishness" (14:29). The truth is that our initial response is often the most destructive. Instead, we should step back, think, and pray to determine the response that will glorify God.

- **Reject the impulse to right every wrong.** Proverbs 26:4-5 tells us both to answer a fool according to his folly and to refrain from doing so. Those who respond to every poke or slight reveal through their lack of self-control that their anger is outrage rather than righteous anger. Trying to correct all the wrong in the world is like trying to empty the ocean with a thimble.

- **Think through what you are trying to accomplish.** Colossians 3:17 says, "Whatever you do or say, do it as a representative of the Lord Jesus." What is your ultimate objective? Righteous anger brings repentance; outrage inflames and divides. While perfectly placed sarcastic comments feel satisfying, they don't serve the Kingdom of God.

1. How often are you quick to respond with outrage? What is it that sets you off? Think through some steps you can follow instead when you start to feel angry.

2. How often do you struggle to let things go? Are you holding
   on to wrongs that you feel people have committed? If you find
   yourself in arguments, disagreements, and conflict regularly,
   think through what is really important versus what you can
   let go.

3. How often are you trying to win the argument rather than
   trying to win over the person? How effective are you at
   listening and responding to others so your disagreements
   end amicably? How can you be more effective in keeping
   God's glory at the center of your disagreement?

Our faith transforms the way we view others. This world tells us
to see others as enemies, but the gospel teaches us to engage even
those who hate us.

> You have heard the law that says the punishment must
> match the injury: "An eye for an eye, and a tooth for a
> tooth." But I say, do not resist an evil person! If someone
> slaps you on the right cheek, offer the other cheek
> also. . . .
> You have heard the law that says, "Love your neighbor"
> and hate your enemy. But I say, love your enemies! Pray
> for those who persecute you! In that way, you will be
> acting as true children of your Father in heaven.
> *MATTHEW 5:38-39, 43-45*

4. How can our willingness to love our enemies impact our witness? How does it point to Jesus?

5. Think about a time when someone was hostile or angry to you and you responded with outrage. How did that affect the situation? Contrast that with a time when you responded with love and forgiveness.

6. When was the last time you prayed for those who have wronged you? List two to three people or groups you feel anger toward. Commit to praying for these people or groups throughout the week.

More than simply not being angry, Christians are called to be angry *at the right things* and *in the right way*. We are called to be angry about sin in our world, most often by standing up to the wicked on behalf of the oppressed. Through such anger, Christians demonstrate an understanding of the destructive powers of sin and the holiness of God.

7. What are sins that we should be angry about? (Consider Isaiah 44:6-20; Jeremiah 7:1-8:3; John 2:13-22.)

8. How have you done at being *properly* angry about the sins you listed above? Do you struggle more with letting your anger turn to outrage or with becoming apathetic and dull?

9. What are ways you can translate anger at injustice and sin into caring for and serving others? As a group, consider practical ways you can show your anger toward sin and engage your community to help remedy the wrongs you see around you.

PRAYER PROMPT

As you close your time together, spend time praying through your struggle with anger and outrage. Ask God for wisdom and self-control to resist the temptation toward human anger and instead to be properly moved to mission by the sin and wrongs of this world.

How Do We Engage the World?

Aligning Our Online Life with Gospel Mission

- For a deeper understanding of speaking effectively into our culture using online tools, read chapter 10 of *Christians in the Age of Outrage.*

- The teaching video for this week's session is available for purchase at https://edstetzer.com/christians-at-our-best.

IN A RAPIDLY INTERCONNECTING WORLD, Christians have never had more opportunities to engage our world with the gospel. Yet this also presents challenges: How do our online habits, attitudes, and relationships reflect our profession of faith? Scripture calls us to be intentional in our actions, being mindful of how they either advance or defame the gospel. What models are we following?

In this session, we will examine how we use digital tools and consider whether we need to reformulate any habits so we bring glory to God rather than add fuel to the world's outrage. Discipleship is just as important online as it is in person, as God calls us to bring our whole being into alignment with his gospel mission.

RECAP AND RESTATE

Use the space below for notes on the key takeaways from the teaching video.

With the rise of social media and other online platforms, we are experiencing a technology _____ gap.

The six principles of digital discipleship are:

1. Remember: _____ is _____.

2. Choose _____ over _____.

3. Make _____ the _____ _____.

4. See _____, not _____.

5. Resist the _____ to _____ every battle.

6. Value _____.

CONSIDER

How do you use social media? Do you use it primarily to talk to close friends and family, or do you talk to others on issues related to your faith? If you don't engage others online, what is it about social media that makes you hesitant to do so?

REFLECT

In Colossians 3, Scripture calls us to a specific way of living as people in Christ, whether online or in real life.

> Since you have been raised to new life with Christ, set your sights on the realities of heaven, where Christ sits in the place of honor at God's right hand. Think about the things of heaven, not the things of earth. . . .
>
> Now is the time to get rid of anger, rage, malicious behavior, slander, and dirty language. Don't lie to each other, for you have stripped off your old sinful nature and all its wicked deeds. Put on your new nature, and be renewed as you learn to know your Creator and become like him. . . .
>
> Since God chose you to be the holy people he loves, you must clothe yourselves with tenderhearted mercy, kindness, humility, gentleness, and patience. Make allowance for each other's faults, and forgive anyone who offends you. Remember, the Lord forgave you, so you must forgive others. Above all, clothe yourselves with love, which binds us all together in perfect harmony.
> *COLOSSIANS 3:1-2, 8-10, 12-14*

1. How should our role as Kingdom ambassadors influence our online behavior? Why might we be tempted to be harsher or more dismissive of people online than we would in person?

2. How does this passage give us a blueprint to effective online engagement? How do the six principles of digital discipleship relate to the ideas in this passage?

3. Paul starts off with the reminder that we "have been raised to new life with Christ." How should this affect our posture toward others online?

4. Why is Christ's peace in our hearts necessary for the kind of love we're called to show? How have you experienced this peace, and how has it helped you engage others, either online or in person?

If we want to use technology and social media as tools for God's Kingdom, we need to practice the six principles of digital discipleship (discussed further on pages 236–243 of *Christians in the Age of Outrage*). Read through the verses that accompany each principle and reflect on what Scripture says about online engagement that glorifies God.

Remember that everyone is watching: 1 Thessalonians 4:9-12; Romans 2:22-24

Choose investment over consumption: Psalm 39:4-5; Matthew 6:19-21

Make grace the default mode: Colossians 4:5-6; Luke 6:32-36

See people, not avatars: Romans 12:10; Luke 18:9-14

Resist the urge to fight every battle: Proverbs 12:18; 15:1; Matthew 5:9

Value truth: Exodus 20:16; 1 John 3:18

5. Which of these principles do you struggle with in your own online activities? Why has this proven to be such a challenge? Where have you found success? What habits or perspectives have you adopted that have helped?

6. Consider your online habits throughout the day. During what activities or on which devices do you find it difficult to exercise these principles? What can you do to put these principles into action?

DIG DEEPER

One of the hardest parts of digital discipleship is recognizing the way our technological habits may hurt our faith and witness. Too often we excuse or downplay their impact on others. Christians can easily fall into one or more of the following destructive online habits:

- **Hollow advocacy:** Content with the perception of service, support, and activism without the sacrifice, Christians tweet or post their thoughts and prayers about issues or causes without ever getting involved. Showing up digitally may signal our agreement, but it ultimately proves hollow when compared with getting involved personally.

- **Anonymous trolling:** The model for conflict resolution in Scripture is to engage with openness, humility, grace, and directness. When we hide behind faceless avatars or create anonymous blogs from which to lob projectiles at church leaders or those on the other side of social issues, we forfeit any righteousness in our criticism.

- **Never negative:** Some well-intentioned Christians mistakenly believe that no one should say anything remotely negative. Ever. However, as we've seen, Christians need to speak up about injustice, oppression, and sin. We need to be cautious, thoughtful, loving, and courageous in speaking the truth.

- **Insta-rage:** Taking no time to think, some Christians lack discernment, self-control, or grace when they post online. They often see everything as the worst. Whether commenting on society, the church, or politics, they are always ready with an insult and rush to judgment.

- **Attention seeking:** Little thought is given to whether what they are saying is true, constructive, or good; the point is to generate as much attention as possible. The question attention seekers constantly ask themselves is *What will get me likes?*

- **The political obsessive:** Whether they take the progressive or conservative viewpoint, these Christians write as if each event is *everything* to them. More troubling, sometimes they interweave their political beliefs with theology as proof that disagreeing with them is disagreeing with God.

1. Which of these patterns do you struggle with? Why might this behavior hurt your witness?

2. Have you ever found yourself in an argument or conflict online? Have you ever unfollowed someone because of their behavior? What caused you to cut off engagement?

3. How can we move from hollow advocacy to genuine service? What are some ways we can move beyond merely raising awareness on social media and online platforms to engaging communities around issues?

4. What are some other online behaviors that you find unhelpful or even detrimental to your mission as a Kingdom ambassador? What are some ways we can lovingly help one another see behaviors that are counterproductive?

From the introduction of the printing press to the Internet, the church has a long history of fighting against as well as embracing major technological innovations. In *Christians in the Age of Outrage*, I focus on the first example of technology as a religious disruptor: the roads of the Roman Empire.

> As the Roman Empire expanded more than two thousand years ago, one of the first things the military did was build roads, bridges, and milestone markers. We take such public infrastructure for granted today, but it is difficult to overstate how this innovation of well-constructed, measured, and protected roads transformed Western civilization. Standardized transportation drastically accelerated the pace at which people, trade, and information could move. It also facilitated the rapid cultural blending process by which Rome exported their language, culture, and religion throughout their new empire. . . .
>
> An unintended consequence of this network was the unprecedented expansion of Christianity. Not only did roads enable missionaries to travel faster, but because the roads were guarded by troops from the Roman army, early Christians were protected from the common dangers of travel that for centuries had restricted rapid movement.

Page 48

Technology is inherently neither good nor bad. Like the Roman roads, every technological innovation is a tool that God has provided and becomes more powerful with each generation. Our mistake is in thinking that Christians do not need discipling in how to use these tools wisely.

5. The example of Roman roads demonstrates the power of new technology to drastically change our lives. How has

technology changed your life? What is different today from twenty or thirty years ago?

6. Unless we intentionally submit our technology use to God, we allow ourselves to be discipled by the world. What practices have you consciously implemented around technology and online behavior? How have these practices changed how you interact online compared to the way the world does?

7. How have you seen technology used for the advancement of God's Kingdom? What churches, ministries, or leaders are using technology in ways that have helped you or others in their spiritual walks? What do they do that makes them successful?

RESPOND AND ENGAGE

Having focused a lot on destructive behavior that can hurt our gospel witness and our own spiritual walk, we need to think critically about the characteristics of a *faithful online presence*. As we begin to think of qualities in those we follow or in our own online behavior, let me offer five qualities for us to consider.

- **Encouraging and edifying:** Rather than imparting a fake positivity, these Christians leave you with important practical truths you can incorporate into your life. Look for those who regularly share articles or videos with real benefits for your spiritual walk.

- **Loving and kind:** These Christians are quick to offer words of support, verses of Scripture, and prayer. They make sure that others are noticed and drawn into community. Even when others respond in anger or hostility, they are civil and demonstrate self-control by walking away in grace.

- **Missional and engaging:** These Christians are not afraid to engage the world with the gospel, bringing their faith to bear in ways that are both winsome and courageous. The answer to outrage cannot be to run away and hide; rather, we must learn how to present the gospel in love without allowing disagreements to devolve into arguments.

- **Charitable and forbearing:** These Christians demonstrate grace and respect, even for those with whom they disagree. Without becoming defensive, they clearly and convincingly explain why they disagree with another worldview or theology.

- **Challenging and humble:** Listening to Christians from different traditions, cultures, and political affiliations is crucial in order to get outside our online bubbles. Humble Christians listen with discerning minds and hearts, and they are open to criticism from people who can point out their blind spots. They exude humility and are ready to admit where they themselves are wrong. It's not worth following Christians who criticize others but are never willing to accept rebuke themselves.

1. Think about people you follow or engage with on social media. What categories would you put them in? What categories of people are you missing?

2. Which of these categories best describe your online engagement? How do you engage others in ways that reflect these qualities?

3. Which of these categories do you struggle to live out consistently online? How can you begin to incorporate these attitudes into your life?

4. What technology and social media habits do you have that do not contribute to your walk or witnessing? Part of hitting refresh is recognizing when certain tools are not cultivating these qualities in your heart. Pray about whether God is asking you to drop them or reform them in service to his Kingdom.

PRAYER PROMPT

Before ending, spend time praying about your digital discipleship. Ask God for the wisdom and discernment to cultivate online habits and attitudes that reflect your life in Christ and testify to the glory of God's Kingdom.

How Do We Engage Our Community?

Recognizing the Power of Thinking Locally

.

- For a deeper understanding of impacting others with the gospel through our daily interactions, read chapter 11 of *Christians in the Age of Outrage.*

- The teaching video for this week's session is available for purchase at https://edstetzer.com/christians-at-our-best.

ONE OF THE MOST SIGNIFICANT yet overlooked ways for Christians to be at our best is to intentionally engage with the people around us. Regardless of who they are, we are to persist in our love toward them, welcoming them into our homes and lives as Christ showed his love for us (Hebrews 13:1-2). The needs of our world are often overwhelming, but Christians can make the most enduring impact by engaging our community with the gospel.

In this session, we will explore how we can have a significant impact on the world by faithfully serving our neighbors. At a time when we are more globally interconnected than ever, it is a countercultural truth that God calls us to think locally.

RECAP AND RESTATE

Use the space below for notes on the key takeaways from the teaching video.

Missionaries of grace . . .

1. Understand that thinking _____ is

   thinking _____.

2. Lay down their _____ and _____.

3. Are _____ to serve _____

   _____ _____ _____

   _____ _____.

Gospel-translating communities are . . .

CONSIDER

Describe how well you know your neighbors. How did you meet them for the first time? How did you get to know them better? (Or what would be a way to get to know them better?)

REFLECT

In 1 Thessalonians, Paul commends the church for their example in living out their calling in their community:

> You received the message with joy from the Holy Spirit in spite of the severe suffering it brought you. In this way, you imitated both us and the Lord. As a result, you have become an example to all the believers in Greece—throughout both Macedonia and Achaia.
>
> And now the word of the Lord is ringing out from you to people everywhere, even beyond Macedonia and Achaia, for wherever we go we find people telling us about your faith in God. We don't need to tell them about it, for they keep talking about the wonderful welcome you gave us and how you turned away from idols to serve the living and true God. And they speak of how you are looking forward to the coming of God's Son from heaven—Jesus, whom God raised from the dead. He is the one who has rescued us from the terrors of the coming judgment.
>
> *1 THESSALONIANS 1:6-10*

1. Paul says that the gospel was "ringing out" from the Thessalonian church into their community and beyond. What is your reputation in your community? How would your neighbors describe their interactions with you? If they had to explain what you are all about, what would they say?

2. What is your church's reputation within its community? When you mention to non-Christians where you go to church, what reaction do you get?

3. The Thessalonian church was an example of faith despite intense suffering. How can suffering (our own and the suffering of those in our community) provide a way to live out our Kingdom mission to our neighbors?

4. The Thessalonian believers followed Paul's example. Who do you know who lives out their Kingdom mission to their neighbors? What do they do that is so effective? Which of their practices can you incorporate as you engage your neighbors?

DIG DEEPER

More than individually living out the gospel, Christians are called to create "gospel-translating" communities, bringing the message of Christ into their unique contexts by going out and welcoming others in. What does that look like where you are? In *Christians in the Age of Outrage* (pages 262–266), I outline five necessary qualities of local churches, summarized below:

- **A community of truth:** While our culture encourages people to "find their truth," the church is called to hold fast to the Christian faith (Titus 1:9). *We* do not define truth, but rather find it in the person and work of Christ. The church is to shape our thinking, sharpen our worldview, and enliven our faith while also making us effective translators of the gospel to a truth-starved world.

- **An embedded community:** If we are Kingdom ambassadors, local churches are Kingdom embassies. The gospel takes root and shape in every culture precisely because it is inherently translatable. Churches need to intimately understand the needs of their community, actively showing and sharing the love of Jesus as they interact with and serve their neighbors.

- **A community of equipping:** Local churches are spiritual hospitals, healing those who enter by preaching God's message of reconciliation into their pain. But it does not end there. Churches are then to equip believers to go out into their neighborhoods as mature believers in the faith (Ephesians 4:11-12).

- **A community of accountability:** Comprised of believers with a common Kingdom mission, local churches are called to be safe places for accountability. When sin is confessed and confronted in love and forgiveness, the church allows for challenging conversations about cultural and social blind spots between members. While most people declare, "I can

say what I want," believers recognize that they are accountable to and a reflection on one another.

· **A community of hope:** During both trials and victories, the
local church reveals that our hope is set on Christ's Kingdom.
That is why we bear with one another, serve one another,
and pour into one another. This hope defines how we see
and engage the world, setting the church apart and drawing
others to Christ.

1. How can the local church communicate the hope and truth
   in Jesus' Kingdom to our friends, neighbors, coworkers, and
   family? What can a community do that an individual cannot?

2. What are your church's strengths and weaknesses in terms of
   practicing the five qualities of a gospel-translating community?

3. Think about the community or neighborhood your church
   is in. What are the unique needs around you? How can your
   church meet these needs?

4. As communities of accountability, our local churches
   are called to be places where we find the conviction and
   encouragement we need to live out our faith. Reflect on a
   time when you have experienced this accountability. How
   did this affect your faith?

The move from simply being a neighbor to really neighboring
begins with intentionally serving others, welcoming them into
our lives, and engaging them in their own. Throughout Scripture,
we are called to practice hospitality. In the Gospels, Jesus set the
precedent by dining with religious leaders and sinners alike. In his
survey on the importance of hospitality in Scripture, Joshua Jipp
offers this important definition:

> Hospitality is the act or process whereby the identity
> of the stranger is transformed into that of guest. While
> hospitality often uses the basic necessities of life such
> as the protection of one's home and the offer of food,
> drink, conversation, and clothing, the primary impulse
> of hospitality is to create a safe and welcoming place
> where a stranger can be converted into a friend.[8]

If we want to engage a hostile and angry world, one of the most
practical yet profound steps we can take is to offer hospitality and
open our lives to those around us as God first welcomed us into his
own family through his Son. As our increasingly interconnected
world struggles with loneliness and isolation, this move toward
intimacy is more important than ever. As you read the following
verses about hospitality, reflect on what each tells us about the
importance of opening up our lives to those around us.

Matthew 25:34-40

Hebrews 13:1-3

Leviticus 19:33-34

Romans 12:20

1 Peter 4:8-10

5. What does Scripture say about the reason Christians should practice hospitality? What is the relationship between hospitality and the poor, the needy, and strangers? Why is this such an important part of the Christian walk?

6. Practicing hospitality can be a struggle because it means opening up and making ourselves vulnerable. How can our faith help us overcome this obstacle? Why does being vulnerable help us engage others?

7. Reflect on a time when a believer practiced hospitality toward you (took you out for a meal, gave you a bed to sleep in, invited you over for dinner). How did that affect your relationship? What did you learn from the experience?

RESPOND AND ENGAGE

Even though most Christians recognize the need to engage their neighbors with the gospel, we can struggle to break through the awkwardness and discomfort that prevent us from reaching out. Yet Jesus calls us to the act of neighboring; that is, to welcome and connect with strangers with the aim of transforming them into friends.

In *Christians in the Age of Outrage*, I outline two practical steps that my wife, Donna, and I took to be more intentional about thinking locally in our Kingdom mission. When we recognized that we wanted to do more to reach our neighbors, we drew a map of our neighborhood, adding notes about what we knew about each neighbor. We began looking for reasons to invite those who didn't know Christ into our home. In addition to cookouts, kids' play-dates, and Super Bowl parties, we began a home Bible study and rejoiced when one couple trusted Christ and began leading a study in their own home:

> Our efforts to reach out to our neighbors began with this map, giving us a reason to discover who our neighbors actually were. It became fun! The key was that we sought to intentionally neighbor our neighbors. We oriented our lives, our actions, and the rhythms of our household and personal relationships around getting to know them, and the map kept that goal at the forefront of our minds. It represented not just some things we did, but the people we became: missionary neighbors.

Pages 275–276

1. Use the following template (a tear out version is available on page 79) to map your neighborhood. Fill in the names of the nearby residents you know. For houses you don't know, make a plan to fill in the blanks over the coming weeks as you engage your neighbors.

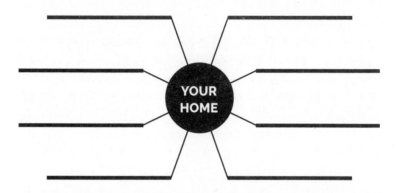

2. We used parties, cookouts, and playdates as opportunities to build relationships with neighbors. Think through what events might be applicable to your neighborhood. What kinds of activities would you want to attend if one of your neighbors invited you?

3. As we planned get-togethers with our neighbors, Donna and I focused on how "Christianese" language can often obscure the gospel and make non-Christians feel like outsiders. What kinds of *insider* language or behavior should you avoid? How

can you convey the same ideas but in ways that would reso-
nate with the language and culture of your neighbors?

4. Because the church is supposed to be a central part of our
thinking locally, how might you involve your church in this
process of building relationships with those on your map?

The second step Donna and I took to move mission from the theoretical to the practical was to keep and update a list of our connec-
tions. We made a list of everyone in relational and professional
proximity to us and our family—coworkers, friends, acquaintances,
and extended family. We added notes to the list as we learned more
about each person, which enabled us to pray for and reach out to
them. As I explain in *Christians in the Age of Outrage,*

> You might see some of these people only once or twice a
> year, and you might see others every day, but having and
> keeping a list will help you take next steps consistently
> and regularly to minister to your family and friends.
> Remembering names and personal details will help you
> neighbor better. Keep this list in front of you by placing it
> next to your bed, on a bathroom mirror, or in your Bible,
> as I do. It reminds me to pray for the people on my list as I
> read Scripture. I'm more likely to find connections during
> the day because my heart is attuned to the opportunity.

Pages 276–277

5. The following illustration is a sample of a list someone might use to intentionally engage with the specific people in their community. Use the tear out version on page 79 to create your own list, including brief details you can pray through and remember when engaging them in the future.

Kathy Jones—employer   ☐ Pray ☐ Engage ☐ Invite

Tim & Mary Chung—PTA   ☐ Pray ☐ Engage ☐ Invite

Lamar Shields—coworker   ☐ Pray ☐ Engage ☐ Invite

Alex Fredricks—Amy's soccer coach   ☐ Pray ☐ Engage ☐ Invite

Omar & Yasma Khan—new neighbors   ☐ Pray ☐ Engage ☐ Invite

6. The key point is incorporating this list into the rhythms of everyday life, remembering to pray and update it throughout the day and/or week. How can you build in time to pray for the people on your list? Where can you put the list to make sure you don't forget about it?

7. In writing out your list, think through specific ways you can demonstrate hospitality toward each person. What would be an effective way of opening your life to them?

As you complete this study, look back over your notes for all six sessions and use these next two questions to consider how you can live out this study over the next few months. God calls us to not simply be repositories of knowledge but to put into practice the truth that he teaches us through his Word.

8. Of what you've learned, what do you think will produce the biggest change in your life? What new habits are you most excited about putting into practice?

9. What do you hope your online and in-person interactions will look like a year from now?

PRAYER PROMPT

Before ending, spend time praying about your neighborhood. Ask God to give you boldness and compassion to move from being neighbors to actively neighboring. Pray through the houses on your map and the names on your list, asking that God would create an opportunity for you to preach the gospel and to build relationships with those he has put on your heart.

Community Map and
List Templates

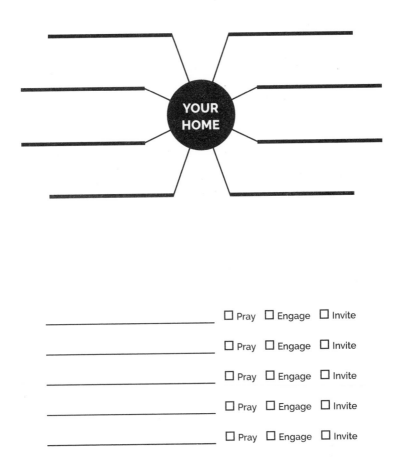

YOUR
HOME

_____ ☐ Pray ☐ Engage ☐ Invite

_____ ☐ Pray ☐ Engage ☐ Invite

_____ ☐ Pray ☐ Engage ☐ Invite

_____ ☐ Pray ☐ Engage ☐ Invite

_____ ☐ Pray ☐ Engage ☐ Invite

Facilitator's Guide

IN MATTHEW 9:36, Jesus is moved as he looks at a crowd, which he compares to sheep without a shepherd. They lack a leader to guide, correct, encourage, and teach them about the right way forward. As the church enters the age of outrage, we need leaders who are committed to engaging our hostile world with the gospel of Jesus Christ.

So let me begin by thanking you for heeding Jesus' call to shepherd his people. While often overlooked, small group leadership is an essential and powerful part of a Kingdom-building church. It is the front line of discipling God's people, a place where sin is confessed and fruit produced in the lives of believers. I am deeply thankful for your willingness to step out in faith and put into practice God's call to feed his sheep (John 21:17).

This study guide was written to help Christians learn how to be their best in a world that has turned against them as it attempts to deal with technological, political, and cultural change. As a result of these pressures, people are lashing out in anger and bitterness. Into this brokenness, the gospel shines even brighter, although many Christians struggle to understand and live out their faith in the face of such hostility. Over six sessions, the study guide unpacks the why and how of cultural engagement in the age of outrage, encouraging Christians not to give in or give up.

This facilitator's guide is designed to offer some helpful advice in getting the most out of the group discussion. As a group leader, you should read through this guide prior to beginning the study and prayerfully consider its suggestions as you facilitate your group.

Advice for Leading

Leading a small group study is an important responsibility. You are entrusted with the spiritual guidance of the group, directing each member to translate the teaching from the video and study guide into substantive opportunities for mutual ministry. On a more practical level, your job is to ensure that the discussion remains focused and fruitful. The following are ways to help make that happen.

Model listening

A small group fails when it is merely a collection of individuals waiting for their turn to talk. An important measure of your group's success, then, is how well each member listens to the others. Listening is actively hearing, understanding, reflecting on, and responding to the words of those around us. At its heart, listening is a fundamental act of valuing others.

You can model real listening by asking follow-up questions. This demonstrates that you have heard and considered what participants said and are inviting them and the entire group to develop the thought further. By actively listening and responding, you will keep the discussion going and allow the group to push past easy and superficial answers for meaningful engagement with one another.

Affirm through repeating

When group members make insightful points or observations, make sure you take note. It is easy for groups to simply jump from one point to the next, which may be entirely unconnected from what was previously said. This not only destroys the momentum of the discussion, but it can leave members believing that what they said might have been wrong or irrelevant. Instead, you should encourage the group by singling out important observations as helpful and building on them. You can use phrases like "John made an excellent point in saying . . ." as a way to highlight particular contributions.

Allow for silence

It might be counterintuitive, but leaders need to learn when they should stay quiet. New leaders can fall into the trap of talking too much: Those who are uneasy with periods of silence might jump in quickly rather than giving more reserved members time to engage. Learn to be comfortable with silence and to give your members time to compose their thoughts.

Remember: Disagreement is not conflict

Disagreement in your group can actually be a powerful tool for spiritual growth. It can challenge members to consider their blind spots and help them gain new perspectives. Disagreement for the sake of spiritual growth shows a spirit of mutual love. On the other hand, the objective of conflict is to win the argument. As a leader, you need to ensure that the group is disagreeing effectively and respectfully rather than devolving into arguments.

Rely on God's Word

Leading a group study can be challenging, and leaders may feel ill-equipped to respond to the needs of the group. Remember that you do not need to have all the answers. You are called to lead humbly and faithfully. Your greatest strength will be relying on God's Word when you don't know what to say. Second Timothy 3:16 tells us that God's Word is "profitable for teaching, for reproof, for correction, and for training in righteousness" (ESV). For this reason, the study is filled with Scripture references. Make use of them.

Be a servant leader

In Luke 22:26, Scripture tells us that "the leader should be like a servant." In other words, godly leaders adopt a posture of humility and sacrifice. More than your brilliance, charisma, or eloquence, your willingness to serve by preparing each week will determine how much your group derives from this study.

Preparation

Key to having a fruitful small group session is for leaders to serve their members by preparing beforehand. With any small group, there will be the temptation to wing it. This is not only shortsighted, but ultimately unloving to your group. Leaders need to "set the believers an example in speech, in conduct, in love, in faith, in purity" (1 Timothy 4:12, ESV). Fundamentally, this means going beyond what you ask of others. As a leader you set the tone for your group, and preparation is a crucial first step in this effort. To this end, two steps are key to preparing to lead each session: Pray and preview.

Prepare by praying

Before the meeting, pray for your group and the topic to be discussed. It's best if you can pray for the group multiple times throughout the week, but at least once set aside time to ask that God would open the group's hearts and that he would speak through his people and his Word. Jesus tells us in 1 John 5:14, "We are confident that he hears us whenever we ask for anything that pleases him." If your desire is for you and your group to grow in faith and be equipped to engage your world with the gospel, your requests are in line with God's will. God has promised to hear you and to work in your heart. The first step is simply to lift up your group to God in prayer.

Prepare by previewing

If the first time you are seeing the questions is when you are reading them to your group, your effectiveness as a leader will be significantly hampered. This study purposefully includes an abundance of Bible verses and discussion questions to allow leaders flexibility in determining what works best for their group. Each small group is different, with unique personalities, challenges, and tendencies. By reading through the study beforehand, you can determine what prompts are best suited for your group's needs. Adjust accordingly.

Videos

Each video is about twelve minutes long. In the videos, I introduce the theme of the session and its relevance to Christian engagement and witness. A central Bible verse helps frame the discussion around Scripture, and in-depth teaching shows how we can live out the verse in our communities and churches.

Recap and Restate

Each session in this study guide includes a notes section to help the group follow along as they watch that week's clip. Prompts focus on the main points in the video to ensure that everyone is on the same page at the start of the discussion period. Encourage your group to take detailed notes during the video, writing down ideas and Scripture references that stand out or confuse them. You may sometimes foster a great discussion simply by asking the group about their reflections on the video.

Discussion

After the video, groups will work through four discussion sections. The goal is to move from the theoretical to the practical.

Consider

Every discussion opens with a broad question designed to break the ice and get conversation moving in the right direction. The prompt is a springboard for later discussion, and it is often best to spend a short amount of time on this question.

Reflect

In the second section, the group is asked to reflect on the teaching in the video as well as relevant Scripture passages. To facilitate group discussion, some questions include a number of Scripture references. Leaders are encouraged to ask group members to read the passages aloud. Short Scripture readings are a useful tool to draw out people who may be reluctant to voice their answers to the question prompts.

God's Word is the most powerful tool you can use to facilitate discussion and exhort your group to mature in the faith. However, do not feel pressured to read *every* verse. This study is purposefully designed so you can expand or contract the number of verses you read, depending on the flow of the group discussion and the time available. Make use of the prompts and questions to flesh out the ideas introduced in the video, but do not feel obligated to hit every point. The goal of this section is for the group to have a firm grasp on what Scripture tells us about the themes introduced by the video.

Dig Deeper

The third section leads groups into a deeper discussion of the theme and its implications for our spiritual lives. This moves beyond the video, introducing new ideas or developing earlier ideas more fully while also drawing upon the experiences of the group. This section will often include a small excerpt from my book *Christians in the Age of Outrage* for discussion.

This section fleshes out what it means for Christians to effectively engage a hostile world with the gospel. Take the time to read through this section beforehand to consider what questions might be particularly relevant to your group.

Respond and Engage

The final section focuses on application, with questions aimed at pushing the group to consider how they can live out what they have learned. Leaders should use these questions to ask members what practical steps they want to take over the next few days in light of what they have learned. This section has these types of questions:

- What old habits are you going to put away? What new habits will you put into practice?

- What goals will you try to accomplish this week (for example, share your testimony with one new person, read your Bible every day)?

- What verses would you like to memorize in order to keep the lesson fresh in your thinking this week?

As people respond, it would be a good idea for you to write down their answers and to follow up with them at the next meeting. This demonstrates your investment in the group's spiritual growth and models Christian accountability.

Closing Prayer

Leaders should end each session with prayer, asking for God's strength and guidance in living out what the group has just discussed. The prayer prompts at the end of each session provide brief summaries of the main idea of each chapter. Leaders can also model listening and engagement by referencing key contributions that the group made in discussion.

Ending in prayer reinforces an understanding that God–not our effort–brings about lasting change in a believer. Consider how Paul ends his first letter to the Thessalonians with this prayer:

May the God of peace make you holy in every way,
and may your whole spirit and soul and body be kept
blameless until our Lord Jesus Christ comes again. God
will make this happen, for he who calls you is faithful.
1 THESSALONIANS 5:23-24

In your prayer, acknowledge that transformation in our spiritual walk and our witness comes through the work of God's Spirit through our faith in Jesus and at the sovereign assurance of the Father. The purpose of this study is not to "try harder" or to be nice. Rather, it is to embrace and live out our identities in Christ as his co-laborers in the work of the Kingdom (1 Corinthians 3:9).

Notes

1. Richard J. Foster, *Celebration of Discipline: The Path to Spiritual Growth* (New York: HarperCollins, 1998), 1.
2. Ed Stetzer, "The Epidemic of Bible Illiteracy in Our Churches," *The Exchange* (blog), *Christianity Today*, July 6, 2015, http://www.christianitytoday.com/edstetzer/2015/july/epidemic-of-bible-illiteracy-in-our-churches.html.
3. Charles H. Spurgeon, Sermon #472: "Believers–Lights in the World" (sermon, Metropolitan Tabernacle, Newington, London, September 28, 1862), http://www.spurgeongems.org/vols7-9/chs472.pdf.
4. Melissa Steffan, "Majority of Churchgoers Never Share Their Faith, LifeWay Study Shows," *Christianity Today*, August 15, 2012, https://www.christianitytoday.com/news/2012/august/majority-of-churchgoers-never-share-their-faith-lifeway.html; Joe Carter, "Study: Most Churchgoers Never Share the Gospel," Gospel Coalition, August 30, 2012, https://www.thegospelcoalition.org/article/study-most-churchgoers-never-share-the-gospel/.
5. Ibid.
6. Bob Smietana, "New Research: Americans Pray for Friends, Family but Rarely for Celebrities or Sports Teams," LifeWay Newsroom, October 1, 2014, https://blog.lifeway.com/newsroom/2014/10/01/new-research-americans-pray-for-friends-family-but-rarely-for-celebrities-or-sports-teams/.
7. Christopher J. H. Wright, *The Mission of God: Unlocking the Bible's Grand Narrative* (Downers Grove, IL: InterVarsity Press, 2006), 423.
8. Joshua W. Jipp, *Saved by Faith and Hospitality* (Grand Rapids, MI: William B. Eerdmans Publishing Company, 2017), 2.

About the Authors

ED STETZER, PHD, holds the Billy Graham Distinguished Chair for Church, Mission, and Evangelism at Wheaton College, where he is the dean of the School of Mission, Ministry, and Leadership. He also serves as the executive director of the Billy Graham Center at Wheaton. Stetzer is a prolific author and a well-known conference speaker. He has planted, revitalized, and pastored churches; has trained pastors and church planters on six continents; holds two master's degrees and two doctorates; and has written or cowritten more than a dozen books and hundreds of articles. Stetzer is a contributing editor for *Christianity Today* and a columnist for *Outreach* magazine. He is frequently interviewed for or cited in news outlets such as *USA Today* and CNN. Stetzer lives in Wheaton, Illinois, with his wife, Donna, and their three daughters.

ANDREW MACDONALD is the associate director of the Billy Graham Center Institute. He is also a PhD candidate in historical theology at Trinity Evangelical Divinity School, where he is studying American Christianity. Andrew and his wife, Jenna, live in Wheaton, Illinois, with their two children, Lucy and Micah.

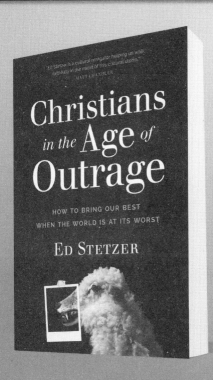